Grow

Lyall Wade

BookLeaf Publishing

Presentation by *BookLeaf Publishing*

Web: www.bookleafpub.com

E-mail: info@bookleafpub.com

ISBN: 9789357740050

First edition 2023

To my family

Dream

Dream the cherished desire
Reach outward and upward, little seed grow.
Enlarge the heart. Be bold! Take courage!
All in, aspire from depth to height
Morning births reality,
labours reward

Look ahead

Dry leaves blanket the ground
Empty branches reaching
Walk on
Have courage
Take a step
Move forward

The path winds away
upwards through the fields
Light soaks the pastures
Dust dances golden in beams
Breathe in
Peace, be still
Take in
beauty, promise, hope

Waves

The waves break on the shore
Tumbling, crashing, rolling, dragging
Constant movement
Constant sound

Blues to whites to greys
and back again
light spots sparkling
wave whistles as it curls
crash on the shore
tumbling up
retreating back
drawing discarded treasures
into the wash again

Reflections

Surface still
images etched
trees beside and upon
not a wind whispers
A pebble is launched
The image is shattered

Cave

you call me
Come out of the dark
Let go of the chains.
No one is holding me here.
Only me.
The cave is devouring.
Dark, pressure, false conflict
paralyse
with half truths and twisted words.
To step out in the light risks
exposure
too bright
stay a while longer
let the tears fall

So tired of this.
Your voice calls again
encourging.
Chains fall from hands
Choose not to pick them up
Leave them behind
Step toward the light
Stand at the cave mouth
Let go of the dark
Set my face to the light

Feel the warmth
Bravely take one step
Just one more

Comfort

Night comes
comforting like a blanket
softly, softly
Owl calls
calm
at home in the darkness.
Look up
stars have been marched out
none are missing
even if me eye cannot see
They retrace their journey
giving direction to the traveller
hope to the lost

Hands full

A mum of three boys
has her hands full
she is told time after time after time.

Their creative curiosity is chaotic expression
never acts of three
rather acts to the power of three

She rides on the waves
of their excited energy
She breathes deep

She stands firm with toes curled and hands
clenched
as they discover new top speeds and higher
highs
Doctors rooms and Emergency rooms are not
unfamiliar

In the shops the endless rows
of pink clothes
raise a smile as fingers reach to touch

Unpacking hand-me-downs
awakens memories

and joy bubbles

Flowers offered in hot dimpled hands
Sweet sweaty faces raised for a kiss
She is their first love

The best mummy in the world
The most beautiful girl
High voices chime we love you lots

Her hands are full
Full of blessings
Full of joy
Full of love

Nanna

I close my eyes and let the memories bubble
along
like water down a mountain stream
tumbling, gurgling, happy
Some memories come quickly cascading
others get caught in the eddies of my mind
hot summer days exploring your garden for fruit
or insects
full blooms roses fulling the air with scent
garden games bridging generations
ice cream melting in bowls faster than it can be
eaten
In the cool of the house
Pa in his chair and you in yours
knitting needles click clack
hand-knitted jerseys in pinks and blues
delicate cups and saucers balance on a tray
with your sweet shortbread
Christmas Eve you fill the house with twinkling
candles
the air is all wax and soft flame
All my childhood filled with love
punctuated by hello darling
scented with breeze soap and perfume

In you

I am your beloved
I am your delight
I am worthy
I am precious
I am known
I am understood
In you I am justified and made righteous
I am sanctified
I am whole

Words

Words have weight
before the wind some blow away
or sting like grains of sand on a beach
Words hurt
with the precision of a warrior's sword or heal
with the precision of a surgeon's scalpel.
Words changes a life, bricks for building or
wrecking ball breaking
Words have power
full of purpose
creating something from nothing

Silence

Silence so deep
there is ringing in the ear
like cicadas dull hum

Shards of shattered ice
cold and sharp
within and without
silence in silence melts

Below water's surface
come up for air
Silently night sky watches.

New to the new

New to the new!
A brand new page turned over
a brand new start
written with your own voice
illustrated with your own choice
You are the masterpiece

Living Life

I am going to start living life
seeking God in the small things
listening for the still whisper
step stepping the spiral
in the rhythms of routines
find worship and joy
following steps of grace
Time to be
restored, renewed
rooted, centred
Breathe in, Breathe out

I m starting to live life
open hands reaching wide
senses receiving creation
inspiration everywhere
allowing joy to rise
steps turn to dance
space to breathe
to receive, to create
a cracking open.
a widening, a response
soul soars on

Dragonfly

Delicate, fragile,
quivering on a blade
intricate, iridescent
held in sunlight
poised ready for flight

Coast

Water exploding
spray in forward, faster, higher.
Wind changing
everything is touches.
Light drawing
a path across the water.
Rock solid
barren appearance deceiving
Life in cracks
Life in pools
Life on shore
Life in sky
Chaos creating calm

Home

Home is one with God, sitting at His hand
White of possibility, of the unwritten on the new
that is good
Spirit pouring out, refreshing, sanctifying
I perch ready strength, beauty in design
Mahala Moya, free spirit
from acorn to sapling to mighty oak
roots sinking deep
peace

African Child

Sky reaches true blue
sun dries the air before a word is spoken

Today children play
blonde heads and brown
skin not too brown
laughter rises
voice chime
'I wrote a letter to my love and on the way I
dropped it'
Easily the game changes
wegkruipertjie, quickly they hide away
Effortlessly language changes

Today children play
at school under desks
the game of terrorist drill
what are terrorists?
dark shadows?

Today children play
van bounces them along
they join children in a ring
skin milky white to dark chocolate brown
smiles as wide as the sky

laughter ricochet
language riot
voices sing
tomatisou sou
feet stamp
hands clap
children dance

children play
games change
change came
childhood mosiac
joyous cacophony

Rise

I see you
sitting in the dust
of brokenness
of disappointment
of pain

Lift your head
They cannot hold you
Rise up
Shake yourself free
You have worth
You have power
For ashes receive beauty.

Fire

flame flickers
wakening flash
tickling tinders reap
growing glow

flames crackle
dart and dash
hypnotic lunge and leap
darkness swallow

flames flicker
to glowing ash
soft orange to sleep
among white glow

Be Still

Be still.
Little one, be still
Rest.
Take a moment
to take it in.
All of it,
every joy,
every hurt,
every burden,
every lightness
every mundane minute
every extravagant experience.

Be still.
Little one, be still.
living is not merely the moving through
moments
moving through days.
Feel the job well done.
Take the warmth of the cup.
See the ones around you.
Embrace the love.
Listen with your whole heart
cracked open wide.
Don't rush on.

This moment will pass
and it will be gone.

Mountain times

Nestled in the foothills
we play
amongst the pine giants
the slopes slippery with needles,
sticky with sap.
The river gurgles over rocks
we look for crabs
float acorn cap boats
leap from boulder to boulder, flying free
the coal from the compound fires fill our noses
Tonight the ink blackness is star-scored.

The mountains encircle us
giant pines smaller than toothpicks
the path winds upwards
under waterfalls to mountain pools turquoise
cool
river becoming stream
the baboon barks and rock rabbits scurry.
Tonight the stars are hidden
the thunder cracks
and echoes
round the mountain rim
lightening flashes, clouds break and rain
downpour.

Tomorrow will be washed bright
and then the night stars will be seen once more.